THE CHOSEN FEW

By:

Jasmine Jones

With Memoirs By:

Xxavier Jones, Matthew Neely, Susan Neely & Justin Willis

THE CHOSEN FEW

Jasmine Jones

ISBN: 978-1-7356265-0-5 (Paperback)
ISBN: 978-1-7356265-1-2 (Ebook - EPUB)

Library of Congress Control Number: 2020920134

Front Cover Art by Timeesha Magnus, Owner of I Am MEE Design
Photo Credits: The Jones Family Archive
Book Design by Arash Jahani
Book Format by Arash Jahani

Printed in the United States of America.
First printing edition 2020.

PhenomenalJas Enterprise LLC
13815 Ginger Lane
Gulfport, Mississippi, 39503

www.phenomenaljasenterprise.com

<u>Dedication</u>

To be told that I could not do something or that I would never amount to anything was nothing but fuel to my fire. I want to dedicate this book to my lovely parents, who raised me and has unfortunately passed on but not before leaving behind an extraordinary legacy, Lonnie Jones, Jr., and Lillie Mae Jones. If ever angels existed on Earth, you two were the perfect example of their glory. I will not forget those that pushed me to do more every day. So, to the naysayers, not even statistics can hold me back because I am in control of my destiny, and I choose to take full responsibility for my life.

My mom and dad that adopted and raised me, Lonnie

Jones, Jr. and Lillie Mae Jones

December 02, 2014

To the Family of Mrs. Lillie Jones

I am very sorry to hear of the passing of Mrs. Lillie Jones. While I have not had the opportunity to personally meet Mrs. Jones nor her husband Lonnie, I have been able to learn of their commitment and dedication to providing a loving, nurturing family environment for children in need of a stable, caring family. Beginning in 1985, Mrs. Jones and her husband were foster parents with Catholic Charities of the Archdiocese of Chicago for nearly ten years. During that time, they welcomed into their family, 17 foster children, and legally adopted 9 of those children, creating a permanent family for them. The children they cared for were of various ages when they entered their home ranging from 3 months old to 13 years old. Welcoming and caring for children who may have come from difficult situations is not an easy undertaking. It requires immense patience and strength of character, the ability to accept children for who they are with all their strengths and challenges, the capacity to provide guidance and stability and it requires a Big Heart. Lillie and Lonnie exemplified exactly that, they welcomed and cared for many children in need of safety, security, stability and Love. On Behalf of Catholic Charities of the Archdiocese of Chicago, please accept my condolences at the loss of Mrs. Lillie Jones who opened her heart and provided love, nurturance, a family and a home to so many children.

Respectfully,

Laura E. Rios

Laura E. Rios, Vice President
Child, Youth and Family Services
Catholic Charities of the Archdiocese of Chicago

THE CATHOLIC CHARITIES *of the* ARCHDIOCESE *of* CHICAGO
651 West Lake Street Chicago, Illinois 60661
Telephone 312.655.7000 TDD 312.236.2800
www.catholiccharities.net

Foreword

I am from the same neighborhood as Jasmine. The south side of Chicago, an area known as "The Jungle" because of how wild it gets at times. God blessed me with a talent, and that was being very good at playing basketball. Basketball kept me out of the streets, but the reason I believe that Jasmine and I made it out of the hood was by being raised in a two-parent household. I am sure we were the few of many in that neighborhood that had both parents under one roof. Jasmine was younger than me, and I spent a lot of time playing with her older brother Richard; but I knew Jasmine was special, kind of like me. Yes, we lived in the hood, but nothing could take away from us smiling daily. I am proud of her, and so happy that my daughter has someone to look up to that comes from my neighborhood.

Yes! We came from the bottom, but now we are on top! I graduated from Duke University, and Jasmine Jones wrote her own book. I truly believe that when you are raised off love, as we were, you tend to feel like you can do anything you put your mind too. Congratulations Jas! I am truly proud of you.

Sean Areon Dockery

No Title Needed

Just A Humble Kid

From the South Side of Chicago

Acknowledgements

First and foremost, I would like to thank my daughter; Heaven Elise Jones, for being my driving force to be a better me daily. With you watching me, I know that I must be extraordinary, you give me no other choice. My godsons: Ryan C. Reese, Jr., and King Rashid Miley, for giving me purpose when I felt as if I could not go any further. To Sheri and Tony Gaskins, Jr., thanks for not only challenging me, but equipping me with the necessities to birth my own book. I would like to go on to thank some phenomenal individuals that have contributed to my vision; Xxavier Jones, Matthew Neely, Susan Neely, Justin Willis, and Sean Dockery with the assist. I appreciate you all for joining me in telling a story that truly never ends. The humility and strength that we all display on a daily basis is the reason that our work will bring about a positive change. Timeesha Hill-Magnus, you completed a puzzle that had so many pieces and yet you were one of the most vital with literally PAINTING my book cover. Victoya Walker, for doing what you do best! Arash Jahani, for rapping up all the loose ends, I am so grateful for you. This journey started back in 2013 and was unfortunately delayed after sustaining so many close deaths. I was able to be pushed by a wonderful support system to continue to persevere. Rebecca Mack, Dave Manson, Kayleen Patrick and the entire Thompson family, Jasmin Pringle as well as the entire Pringle family, Dr. Uvo T. Oghre-Ikanone and the entire family, Taja Hicks as well as the entire family, Dejah Camp, Michael and Keva McNeal, Samuel and Darlene Camp as well as the entire family, Paula Brown and the entire family, Tanesha Stamps, Laverne Johnson, Melissa Parker and the entire family, Mary Nightingale, Marci Deloney, Willie B. Jordan (Granny Gritts), Joan Simpson, Johnathan Krikie, Lawrance Ronreco Kennedy,

Tracey Madden, Tyre Brown, Kelli Smith, Donovan Smith, Mark Terrell, Randall Garrett, Darion "Jake" Anderson, Lamous "Chris" Holliday, Karla Wadley-Grant and the entire family, Lisa Wadley, Tyrese Lindsey, Marcellous Furlow, Tiffanie Benson, Zakkiyah and Matthew Shelton, Jeffrey Higgins, LaQuan Buice, Lachinka Perez, Laketa Buice, Sabrina Baker, Tyron Leftridge, Jeremy Young, Kristy Young, Christopher Parker, Antonio King, Stanson Carter, Andrea Williams, Halston Hallman, Jason Simpson, Yvonne Johnson, Rashonda Lofton, Craig James, Isiah McDaniel, Eunice James, Khalif Karriem, Emmanuel McDaniel, Mary Johnson, Brittany Browder, James Lacey, Linda Diggs, Gloria Ann Mullens, Sharday Stewart (Little Sister), Ryan Westfield, Sherrod Dockery, Charles Tate, Kinette Ingram, Danielle Cross, Stefon Johnson, Deanca Harris, SFC Randolph Steven Adams, Lonnie D. Harrison, Nicole Eggerson, Shacarta Gardner, Gwenda Ingram, Christina Stowers, Bertha Marshall, Christopher Ellis, Bertha Stokes, Ashton & Christina Booker, Rosie

Ingram-Boyd, Kiesha Tigner, Carrie McClendon, Coach Hicks (Esmond Elementary School gym teacher), Nancy Mae Smith, Ms. Rounds (Esmond Elementary 8th grade teacher), Eva Ingram, Betty-Joe Lewis, Henry and Pearlie Ingram, Billy and Rosie Ingram, Johnnie Ruth Conley, Arelius Ingram, Evelyn Ingram, Dr. Keesha Karriem and family, Darnell and Lisa Dean, Rhonda Minor, Jasmine Spencer, Erika Bradford, Phillip Owens Jr., Chaz Owens, Celestine Corrigan, Gary McIntyre, Jr., Joe Frankie III, Daniel Phillips and Spencer Leak, Jr. To my two nephews and niece whom I had the honor of helping to raise; Gary McIntyre, III, Mia Williams, and Laquinton D. Jones; it has been a pleasure being such a positive force in your life, keep pushing me to be a goal digger! Fred Cross, Keisha Boler (Big Sister), Tiffany Boler (R.I.P. Big Sister), Monique Tolliver, Christopher Pitts, Markina Chambers, Shakentha Chambers, Antonio D. Rodgers, Jazmine Rodgers, Lawrence Rodgers, Jeamaire Mitchell, Sharon Thomas, Patsy (Big Sister) and Coach Jesse Chick, Florine

Lewis, Georgia Ann Harris, Karen Hoosier, Brian Hoosier, Gloria Butler, Cathy Rodgers, Jasmine Carroll, Cynthia Beasley, Daniel Beasley, Denzel Beasley, Rashawn "Herb" Pitts, LeRon Williams, Stacey Parks, Abubakr Abdurrab (Big Brother), Chante Jones (Big Sister), Joyce Perry, Ray "JayCo" Weatherspoon, Levonia Small-Weatherspoon, Shannon Elise Johnson, Lee Harper III, Rosie Johnson (Big Sister), Terrell Lofton, Loyal Lofton, "TC" Lofton, Victoria Smith (Big Sister), Stariesha Williams (Little Sister), Joneisha Williams (Little Sister), Maurice Ben, Joy Hanshaw, Christina Betts, Michael A. Smith, Ella Wright, Kristi Pride, Charlotte Terrell, John Davis, Kelly Truitt, Sharhonda Martin, Pamela Flowers, Angela "NeNe" Jackson, Daryl Jackson, Jonathan Ray, Melvin Jones, Posey Jones, Deja Jackson, Daniel Jackson, Daryl, Jr., Laura Head and the entire Head family from out west. Much thanks and blessings to Towanda and Dante Perkins of D.L. Perkins, Sr. Memorial Chapel (The Rolls-Royce of Funeral Homes); in times of loss, your family has provided much relief and great care. To my entire biological as well as adopted family; it is a lot of you all but know that I love every one of you dearly. Sylvia Clayter, Chris Mosley, Shabazz McClellan, John Whitfield, the entire Morgan Park Community, The Forest Preserves of Cook County Conservation and Experiential Programming Department, Esmond Elementary School, West Gulfport Civic Club, Kareem Barker, Daniel Harris, Vera Martin, Christian Dixon, Antoinette Daniels, Sequoya Lewis, Lacreisha Johnson and the entire family, Paris Caruthers, Shaniece Taylor, Jasmine Taylor, Jarrell Perkins, The GTwinz (Justin & Jarrell), Stacey James, Regina Johnson, Brian Pickett, Tracey Madden, Charlotte McLaurin, Councilman Kenneth "Truck" Casey, Fredrick Bass, Patrick Bass, Adrian Davis, Vania Long, Shawnda Saucier, Fredrick Bass, Felecia Spivery, Verdina Sweat, Christy Corbett, Jeffrey Hulum III, Quimby Handy, Jeanine Casey, Denise Dunomes, Attorney Nita Chase, Leila Lang, Taiwana Flowers, and Louis and Martha Gholar. Much respect and love to the city that showed me, life is what you make it, and taught me how to be tough and humble, Chicago. To the City of Gulfport, for embracing me and making me feel right at home. Also, several others that most likely are mentioned within the body of this book. I want you all to know, that I appreciate the love, support, and things that you may not be aware of that enabled me to keep pushing throughout the years. To everyone that has ever been there for me throughout my life, I am forever grateful.

In loving memory of Will Long, an extraordinary being, who was the first person along with his big brother, Jason Long, that me and my siblings met when we moved to Park Forest. Will, your legacy and kind nature will live on through individuals like myself that refuse to allow such a good person to die in vain. Your mom, Rose Long, birthed a legend and the evils of this world took you away from us all, way too soon.

To those that have passed on that I held dear to my heart and who will always occupy my soul. You will live on through me, your legacy will never be forgotten. To the other "Chosen Few"; Lavelle Jones, Angela Jones, Richard Jones, Shonna Jones, Valentino Jones, Vincent Jones and Valon Jones; may this book be the foundation on which we build upon. Most importantly, I would like to thank the Lord God for carrying me through. So many people doubt you, but I cannot live without you! When I should have lost my mind, you have kept me. I have experienced some of the most hideous mental states, circumstances, and situations but you brought me out and I will forever live for you. Only what you do for Christ shall last!

Contents

Introduction

O n a sleepless night, I lie down and contemplate my approach to even begin the task of creating a work of art that depicts me as a person, an individual, and, most notably, a child of God. Growing up in certain situations and facing many obstacles enabled me to strengthen areas that could use an upgrade from weak, it made me stronger. Through a couple of breakdowns that I thought would destroy me, I became indestructible. I never wondered why God allows certain things to happen or life to be fair, harmful, or sometimes wonderful. I just always knew that God had a plan for me, and I always considered myself "The Chosen Few." I apologize to all my Chicago house heads because I am not referring to the shindig you all have each year. I took it upon myself to name an elite group of people from different backgrounds and races with one main thing in common; they entered the system. This system consists of orphans, foster children, and "The Chosen Few," the adopted children. Excuse me if this seems a little harsh; one thing that always made me feel better after finding out that my parents adopted me was that I was chosen out of many and placed with the few, which was a blessing. So, I am lying here in bed, and all these thoughts are culminating, and I realize where I would have to start, and that is where everything began.

My life from my memory started on a block on the south side of Chicago called Church Street. I thought that maybe I would allow the reader into my childhood, then into my teenage years, and finally my "I'm Grown" years because we all know that those are the years that we discuss before we even arrive there and later realize that we had spoken way too soon. I may bounce around a lot in trying to portray my life growing up in what most people would describe as an unfortunate situation, but honestly, being adopted by my mom and dad was the best thing that had ever happened to me. For all the children growing up facing the same obstacle that many other children and I have encountered, I have some important words of advice for you. Accept the present and be grateful that someone else even wants to deal with you. Let's be real, most of us come from some pretty jacked up families, and the people that come along to try to give us some sense of function don't even know what type of dysfunction they may be taking home with them. I am going to discuss my younger years, and the time I wasted being angry at everyone that I could have avoided if I had someone to school me on what I know now. Life is short, and what you do today does affect your tomorrow, but the word mistake is not in the Merriam Webster Dictionary for no reason. I learned from all my mistakes growing up, which is how I was able to adjust to coming of age. I am glad I could experience life with brilliant siblings that just so happened to be adopted along with me. Everybody was different and unique in their own ways. In the home I grew up in, many people came, and many people left throughout the years. That was befuddling, and for those of you who are wondering what the word "befuddling" means, it is just "confusing" in a yes, I am fancy way. I have always desired to aspire to be and do whatever I wanted; even as an adolescent, I had big dreams.

Chapter 1:

A Story Within Itself: The Infamous Book Cover

I got the weight of the world on my shoulders. I could handle it because that is how you get stronger. Searching for love in all the wrong places, instead of waiting for the Lord to give me a true blessing. Why am I stressing? Great heart, brilliant mind, but certain things are not of the essence. I fiend for a life that could wash away my past transgressions, living day by day, hoping someone gets my message. To be free! I came into this world empty-minded, not knowing white from black, wrong from right, or love from hate. October 17, 1986, yes, indeed, this was the date that my life began. Born at Cabrini X Hospital, who am I? Well, I was born Angelina Denise Williams, but life's circumstances had given me the name Jasmine Jones. This by itself made me have an identity crisis growing up. Along with the fact that I had been given the nickname "Doesy". Lord knows I was a confused child. I wanted my book cover to express a story that every individual could tell differently that looks at it. The saying is "a picture is worth a thousand words," right? I am shooting for a million words, which would make this cover art sui generis.

You may have looked at the book cover and thought, "The Few Chosen" instead of "The Chosen Few." Well, just like my book cover, children placed in the system are misunderstood too. If you look at the incubators, the two in the front are three months old and thirteen years old. My parents that raised me legally adopted nine children.

The youngest was three months old when placed in their care, which was me. The oldest was thirteen years old when placed in their care; my brother Lavelle. As my good friend Matt once stated, "older kids are marginalized in the adoption system so it's good to see a thirteen-year-old being adopted". I achieved exactly what I wanted when he also told me that the cover was thought provoking. The incubators represent the parents/system that come along to take care of us, nurture us and raise us to become the adults we are today. It is somewhat like a womb that is dependent on this system.

I have grown into the point where the incubator can no longer hold me, which is why you can see me also standing up against the brick wall representing the present. Surrounded by words that helped me get to the point in life that I am now. On the next pages are pictures drawn by my brother, Xxavier Jones, of the original book cover. I wanted you all to see how such an extraordinary work of art came to be. My brother is currently incarcerated so he had to do the best he could with what he had; to draw an image that I depicted to him. I sent him a stick figure sketched drawing of my vision and my brother was able to draw this. Look at how Timeesha Magnus, with her tremendous talent and gift, brought what my brother had drawn to life. Voila, the book cover! I want the reader to draw their own opinions on this work of art, so I will not expose all the inside scoop. Instead, let us get to the book!

Chapter 2:

Memoirs of an Adopted Kid

In a world full of misfits, we all began to stand out quite well. People can tell many stories about being an adopted child, and I would not provide a comprehensive analysis without exploring some views and actions of someone else. This chapter is just some snippets of a few individuals that were also adopted. Every individual feels different about their experience and subsequently has different viewpoints and words of advice that can and will be of great assistance to those that take heed to what they read.

Adoption

By: Matthew Neely

Adoption can be a difficult subject to deal with. Many children grow up asking the question: why? For this, there is no easy answer. It is difficult for a child to imagine life from someone else's point of view. Especially if that point of view is that of someone that the child sees as infallible and perfect such as a parent. As we get older, we realize that our parents are just like us: flawed and irregular. We recognize that they are only people and not the gods that we idolized as young children. As we begin to understand this, we start to see that sometimes lives are brought into this world by unprepared people to deal with the responsibility. There is a myriad of reasons for giving a child up for adoption, far too many to name here. Often the adopted child can grow to resent their biological parents. It becomes an albatross around many parents' neck that decide to put their children up for adoption. However, many children were saved from a destructive and malignant existence because their parents decided to put them up for adoption. Many people were unable to reproduce that now have a child in their lives thanks to adoption.

I was an adopted child. I have always known this. Both of my sisters were adopted; we were all raised together. We behaved as any other siblings would. We had our share of fights and mischief, but if we did not tell you, you would not know that none of us were blood related. As a child, people often mistook my younger sister and me for twins (a fact that I still shudder about to this day). Sharing similar DNA is irrelevant to being family. Family is a bond that grows through shared experiences and struggles. I am fortunate to have grown up in a loving home.

It was not the best, and I still have issues coming to terms with certain things, but at least it was mine. There are many individuals that were not so lucky.

Furthermore, these are things that I have realized since coming into adulthood. As a young man, I felt disenfranchised and jaded about family. What good was I if my flesh and blood exiled me before I could even walk and talk? I have even had an ex say to me during an argument: "Your own family didn't want you." This penurious statement spoken in ignorance epitomized the way I had felt most of my life. Why didn't my family want me? It was the question that plagued most of my adolescence. It led to me alienating myself from my peers. I felt wrong like I did not belong with the "normal" kids with "normal" families. Looking back now, I realize just how foolish and irrational these thoughts were, but they consumed me at the time. It was tattooed upon my very soul. It was a blight on my existence, a stain that would not wash out. There is nothing more frustrating than needing answers and never getting them to a child. If you know of a child that is having trouble dealing with the fact that they were adopted, you should talk to them. Ensure that they understand that they were not put up for adoption because they lacked love. They were put up for adoption because their parents loved them enough to realize that they could not care for them.

Lost & Found But Still Misunderstood

By: Xxavier Jones

W hat factors do you take into consideration when deciding if someone is family or not? Webster defines family/fam'ie as, 1. Parents and their children, 2. Relatives. Therefore, blood does not necessarily make your family, so blood is not thicker than water as an adopted child. I do not see the point in abiding by society's politically correct terms regarding who I determine to be my family. Such as someone being my adopted, foster, or step relative. Because then you are creating this false sense of familiarity by not necessarily considering them to be your real relative. Using epithet terms such as foster, step, or adoptive relatives title dilutes the term of endearment. Through my Jones family experience, I learned that loyalty and especially love, that real unconditional love. It will be there; no matter what you say, what you do, no matter what happens, period.

I am always going to love you, and you will always be my daughter, sister, brother, son, father, or mother. To me, love is the main component necessary when considering how you see another individual. It was not clear at first; it took some time for me to understand this myself. By the time I reached 112th & Church, the Jones residence, I had a lot of pent up aggravation. It took me a while to realize that harboring on to that negative energy prevented me from moving forward in my life. I had been given a second chance at life, yet I sat dwelling in the negativity of my life circumstances. Instead of persevering through the challenging obstacles, I faced by holding onto faith. My life situation would not be as bad if I had a different perspective on things; sometimes, reluctance and distrust can cause us to be our own worst enemy.

Brutal honesty is the best policy, and this is being brutally honest. Here I stand before you vulnerable, stripped naked to the core of who I am and how I got there. From the moment I stepped into my new foster home, I was afraid and confused. At that time, there were a lot of internal struggles I was dealing with. I felt that I was only skimming the surface of who I was. A lot of adopted kids, including my brothers and sisters, felt like this. I know because I was in the very same predicament. When I looked in their eyes, they reflected mines. We were in the same situation but with different circumstances.

That realization was comforting to me and the others and set me free from the cocoon of fear and confusion that I inhibited. At first, I felt reluctant to open-up, especially after being in several homes before being placed with the Jones's. I was afraid to make that irretrievable leap into the

unknown. After being hurt in the past, I did not know if I could handle the flood of emotions that would pour out if I opened myself up. But their compassion, love, and acceptance helped to concrete the foundation of trust between us. After being disappointed so many times before, they made me believe that beautiful relationships do not have to end in carnage. They showed me through their actions, and that is what love is; it is an action word! When the Jones family adopted me, I was tossed a lifeline. It made me aware of how I had been drowning. Upon arrival, I felt off-balance, aware of something missing, a feeling of emptiness. After being with them for a while, I felt life and strength flowing into me. Making me feel whole again. I was fortunate to have three of the best role models of my life. Who happened not to be biological relatives, even though I loved them as if they were. My father, Lonnie, was a man who positively impacted my life. He gave me my work ethic by teaching me how important it was to work hard at a young age. which opened many doors for me later in life. He also taught me the skills needed to be a man and provide for my own family one day. Another one of my role models was my brother Lavelle who taught me to open my mind and be inquisitive. He created my desire to learn new things, which led to the acquired intelligence level that I have today. Most importantly, he taught me to be proud of my ancestry and myself as a strong black man. Last, but not least, my brother Richie from whom I acquired my sense of style, taste, and basketball love. I was his shadow for so many years and learned so much from him. He single-handedly made one of the biggest impacts of my life. I was also blessed to have beautiful, strong, and smart women in my life, like my adopted mother and my biological grandmother, who played instrumental roles in my development. They made it possible for me to tap into and take advantage of my true potential. Through them, I've learned that I play a very intricate role in my children's lives and plan on using the knowledge that I gained from life experiences to emphasize the importance of choices and help guide my daughters as they develop. Through my life experiences, I have attained knowledge that I plan on passing on to my daughters so that I do not end up with my own little Billie Holiday, another black girl lost. Which brings me to the topic of my biological mother. A woman that I love regardless of what happened, everything I have been through, and strangely, I always will. You do not have to forget, but you must forgive to move on. See, for several years, I got to visit my younger sister and mother at Catholic Charities. Going to visit my biological mother helped but also hindered my progress. It gave me a false sense of hope. It was like having the ultimate prize dangled before my eyes, but just out of my reach. It was the ultimate tease, a concept that I could not quite grasp. During this time, I was experiencing intense and profound feelings of nostalgia that these visits triggered. I felt haunted because every time I closed my eyes, I saw her face as if it were seared on my psyche. The reality of the situation was submerging subconsciously with my deepest fear, and the love I had for her started to turn into resentment. When she stopped visiting me, the residue of her remained whenever I closed my eyes. Pretty soon, the turmoil that I felt inside caused negative reactions in my behavior. I started to shut down by repressing my emotions to cope with my emotional state, which caused red flags that ended with me having to see a psychologist. After displaying symptoms of being emotionally unstable and incapable of showing sentiment, the truth of the matter was that I still felt alone, although people surrounded me. I applaud my mother and father because they could have chosen to throw me back into the foster care system. Which they could have easily done since they had not adopted me yet. Instead, they executed patience and showed compassion by being sympathetic and showering me with love when I needed it the most. At first, my caseworker, Ms. Murphy, would take me to these therapy sessions, but a white man would come to pick me up along with other kids after a while. During many of these sessions, I would be placed in a room with an art easel and told to express how I felt by drawing or painting a picture. Honestly, the reason that I went as long as I did, was that I loved to draw. Plus, I got to buy junk food with the $2 that mommy and daddy gave me when I went. Also, because I had a crush on one of the girls who rode with me to therapy. But once summer rolled around and I noticed that I was the only kid in the family

and neighborhood that went to therapy, I instantly refused

to go any longer by throwing tantrums and hiding when

the van came to pick me up. After a heart to heart with

momma, she reluctantly agreed that I did not need to go

any longer. Believe it or not, me being home was more

beneficial to my state of being than the months of

psychiatric therapy that I received. Being separated from

everything and everyone started to cause me to regress. I

did not understand what was going on. I felt confused and

alone. Anyone that has ever been abandoned knows what it

is like to feel stuck in a state of suspense. It is like being

trapped, stuck in between my past and my future, and not

knowing which one to choose or which way to go.

Eventually, I learned to cope, and my experience became

therapeutic for me; it made me stronger afterward. Even

though I worked through my initial emotional state, I still

felt alone when surrounded by people. I learned that there

was nothing wrong with how I felt. I began to accept the

fact that I am introverted, that I am a loner by nature. Which explains why I would roam around aimlessly and still do to this day. It is funny how something that I thought of for so long as a curse was a gift. It made me observant and helped me to focus, as well. It also helped me to be able to decipher others by providing insight into my situation. Unlike my brothers and sisters and many other adopted kids, I was fortunate to know both sides of my biological family. I was in contact with them from pretty much the beginning, which was another one of the gifts and a curse situation. You would think that having this contact would make my transition easier. Instead, it made things much more complicated for my adolescent mind. I could not comprehend what was going on at that time. The only thing that I was sure of was that I had a younger brother and sister, only because we were all together when I went to visit my biological mother. Another example of how I was more fortunate than other adopted kids was that I had a say in where and who I wanted to stay with. Any other child in my predicament would have elected to stay with their biological family. Still, I chose to stay with the Jones's; because I was told that my biological family only wanted custody of myself and not my little brother. Since we shared the same mother but not the same father and my father's side was fighting for me, I could not leave him. He was the only consistent presence in my life for as far back as I can remember, even after losing the custody battle for me. My biological father's side of the family remained a steady presence in my life. In the end, I got to spend time with my biological family while still be able to stay with my little brother. Having my adoptive and biological family in my life became essential in my development into adulthood. My experience from being in the foster care system has been both bitter and sweet. Overall, I have learned that no matter what our life circumstances may be, we are ultimately the deciding factor in how our life turns out. We can either give up and fall victim to circumstances that are out of our control, or we can decide to use these mishaps as fuel to persevere through our trials and tribulations. There is no such thing as a perfect person or life; searching for either is futile. Instead, we must make the best with what we are given.

I Was Chosen, Too

By: Susan L. Neely

arbara Ann Neely. To a lot of people, that name may
not have that much significance. To me, however, this
is the name of my queen, my provider, my protector, my
cheerleader, and so much more. Barbara Ann Neely is my
mother. I believe that God always directs your path. God's
direction for me led me right to Barbara Ann Neely. I did
not grow inside of her for nine months; she chose me to
be her daughter. Adoption can be a beautiful experience.
It is one thing to bring life into the world, which is a
miracle within itself, it is another thing to decide to go to
an adoption agency and say, "I would like a child." Love

comes in so many different forms, spoken and shown in so many ways. My mother loved me with everything in her. If you were none the wiser, you would have never guessed that I was adopted. DNA was never required in our household. Barbara Ann Neely loved me, hugged me, bugged me, reprimanded me when needed, made sure I had what I needed, hustled for me, and I can go on and on. Though, there were times that I felt different only because I did not know any other adopted children for a long time. On top of that, I was an oddball in school. I look back on everything, and I know that I did not get any less love and acceptance than my classmates, and my mother never made me feel any different. She is my mother, period. Even though she is gone now, I will forever be impacted by her. I honestly do not know what would have become of me if she had not chosen me to be her daughter. Adoption is beautiful. Adoption is enriching. Adoption, a lot of times, is necessary. My mother is my queen forever and ever! No DNA is required.

A Chosen Life

By: Justin Willis

Who am I? The answer to that question may seem easy, but it is not. To tell my story, I must mention something before I began. My path starts with two individuals who met while they were in high school and created me off a bet and lust, not love. I was born on the 7th day of July in the year 1985. My parents never raised me; my grandparents raised me because they agreed to take care of me until my parents finished high school. Well, I guess you know how that turned out. I did not realize until I was older, around eight or nine, that the people who were taking care of me, raising me, was not my mom and dad.

How I found out was a little heartbreaking. The person who I thought was my brother, but who was my uncle, got jealous of a kid getting attention from the people who were his peers and friends, so he told me that I was adopted. At that point, life came to a crashing halt to me, seeing that what you know is not what you think. For years I spent my life trying to live for acceptance and trying to fit in when all became crystal when I reached an adult point in my life. I began to understand that you are not meant to fit in or need to be accepted by everyone, but you are who God intended you to be, so people can like it or not. One of my earliest memories was being in bed with my grandmother, watching Star Trek the Next Generation. Reminiscing of how simple life was and carefree, not a real thought of responsibility. On my first day of kindergarten, I remember it quite well. My grandfather dropped me off to class while he was on his way to work, and I was scared and confused. I had so many questions and no answers. Why is he leaving me here? Who are all these other people? Who is the big person? What is going on? I was scared. But as I got older in life, that fear turned into a form of strength that would help me venture into the unknown and allow me to be the man I am today. During my years in grade school, I was a lot shorter than my classmates, but that was my source of what made me want to drive harder than anyone else. While I received an unlimited amount of love from my grandparents, I often felt left out from my other relatives as if I was the extra child who shouldn't be there, but after time, I got used to it.

Chapter 3:

Everything Is Not Always Peaches & Cream

In life, you learn many things, and only through experience do you begin to formulate living. I have always been a perfectionist, but clearly, nothing and nobody is perfect. My thought process was to try to be as close too perfect as possible, and it seemed as if those same standards for me were held by my parents that raised me. I seemed to be doing well on the outside, but I always

have fought a mental battle to cope with the cards that life had dealt me. It was as if I was playing poker, but the only card game I was familiar with was spades. My mother was always nagging me about things that I felt were not necessary and why I should not do certain stuff. Growing up, it pissed me off that she did not mind her own business, but eventually, I came to realize that she knew that I not only deserved better but that much better and greater was in store for me. When you cannot recognize and see your possible downfalls, others in your life can, and for me, it was my mom and dad.

I loved both my parents dearly, and I showed them that daily but that still did not mean that we agreed on everything. Some disagreements were much more intense than others leaving both parties to repent and ask each other for forgiveness, and some were simple and more bearable and easily forgettable. I learned that when someone, especially your parents, wants the best for you and knows that you are destined for greatness that everything is not always peaches and cream. My parents told me the truth no matter how mad or upset it would cause me to get, they never sugar-coated, or water downed anything, except Kool-Aid. Perfection depends on perception; I have learned that veracity communication is the best resolution for most issues. I have fallen out with a few people that I considered to be close friends over the years because of misunderstandings, but I was not about to call them if they did not contact me because of pride. Hell, it was their fault anyway. That is most likely the same thing they were thinking though. You still need to give a person a chance to explain what you may not have fully understood and try to provide the closure needed to move on or mend things. For the people that common sense is not so common amongst, just let them continue to bask in their irrational understanding. Now, some stuff you cannot even give some people a chance to come back from. With certain individuals, it is just best to leave them completely alone. I am referring to the toxic people you find yourself constantly forgiving, but they continue to do you wrong and cause confusion in your life. Give it to God; they may deserve a special place in Hell, with a first-class ticket with gasoline draws/panties on arriving there; but don't you go being their main sponsor to provide what may be considered a luxurious trip for them. My godmother, Mama Pam, has always been a big inspiration to me. What I have loved most about her is that she exemplifies the title of this chapter. Pamela Ward is a wonderful woman that has grown through so much but has persevered through it all. She has always been blunt with me, and during my second break down, it was her reality check that helped me restore my mind. She did not speak to the weak me; she spoke to the strong and zealous me. You go through stuff, and it is beneficial to deal with it, but after doing so, suck that mess up and keep moving forward. Life goes on, with or without you. Her son is my best friend, and no matter what happens in either one of our lives, he will always be that. We had become so close throughout the years that we know each other overly well. Although I was the operation's brains and muscle, he was the test monkey that had some excellent advice when you needed it. All jokes aside, Ryan C. Reese, Sr., has always exhibited traits that I could never acquire. It is merely because we are and have always been two different people. He has always had the ability not to care or show that he cared about things that would bug the hell out of most people. I, on the other hand, have always cared too much. It is good to have friends that are not like you because that balance is needed in your life. Friends that are not afraid to call you out on things but most importantly, friends who love is unconditional. My father, who raised me, was the same way; if it was not about his household, it did not concern him. You must be like that sometimes, if you want to survive in a world that vultures exist. In my adult life when an overflow of responsibility was placed on me. I figured that my best friend would be there and understand without me having to explain. I became angry with him because after losing both of my parents; I felt like he did

not reciprocate the same things as I did when it came to

our friendship. I later realized that my expectations were

kind of high and somewhat unrealistic. He was getting

his life together, as I thought about what had transpired

in that of my own that had been devastating. At the time,

he was in the academy to become a Chicago police officer,

and although a lot of people frown upon cops; Ryan had

been a bystander to violence throughout his life that

gave him purpose especially within the career in which

he performs with dignity and a courageous heart today.

Growing up without his father gave him the incentive to be

an extraordinary one. He experienced seeing a close friend

get his brains blown out right in front of him. As I pulled

up on the block that day, he walked across the street from

the home that it had just occurred in and told me what

transpired. He fell to his knees. As I stood there watching

him kneel down in pain and disgust, he looked up at me

with tears in his eyes and in the midst of the turmoil, he

said, "Doesy, when I become a police officer I'm going to get all these guns off the street." We both have tried hard to make our word our bond, so I have no doubt that he is diligent in trying to do his part in combating the violence that happens on the streets of Chicago daily. When some of you run around yelling, "F**k 12", "them PIGS ain't s**t" or whatever. Keep in mind, that a lot of these officers took the oath to serve and protect and come to work each day, to do just that. Just like we all go to work every day and yearn to make it back home safely to our family, so do they. We all have a common goal and although it is easy to say what you would or would not do in an instance. You would never know until you are put in that situation. What is blatant with no disregard has been quite clear and is unpalatable but let us not fly off the hinges so quickly at everything that takes place. By the way, this is coming from someone that has been a victim of police brutality. I had my elbow fractured by a Park Forest police officer in my junior year of high school. I do not even believe that he was reprimanded and because my parents were not that privy when it came to certain things, nothing at all was done. It made me hate the police with a passion, but it wasn't until my biological family found me, seeing that I had terrific siblings that were Chicago Police Officers also, that my outlook on Five-0 changed. It enabled me to begin to rid myself of the fear and anguish that this officer had caused. It is not good to allow anyone to hold a negative precedence in your life because of their actions. I had to improve for me.

Chapter 4:

On My Lonesome

T hey say that "blood is thicker than water", but most people fail to realize that this statement is only true in a physical sense. Blood runs through all our bodies and without water our bodies could not survive. The household that I was raised in consisted of nine adopted children and several foster children. Everybody in the house that was adopted had a biological sibling with them, except me. So, I found myself feeling lonely many times especially when we encountered disagreements, and everybody seemed to team up with their biological sibling

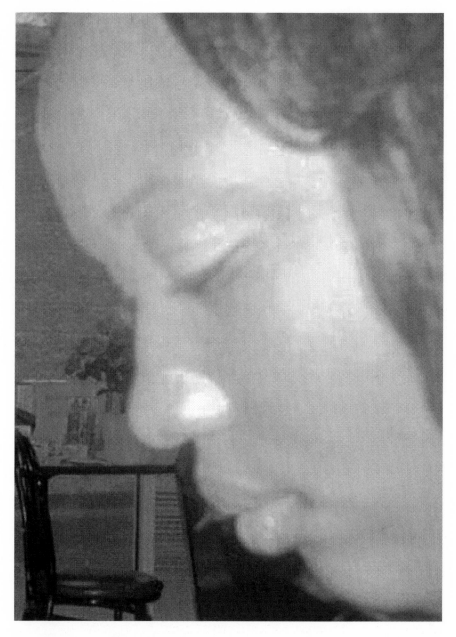

or siblings. This desolate loneliness enabled me to become

stronger physically, mentally, and emotionally because it

forced me to rely on myself more than on others. When you can just sit back and observe instead of running your mouth, things become clearer. I was forced to notice the situations in my life that created a fierce force inside of me that commanded me to be great, to be strong, to be resilient, to be humble, to simply be me. You begin to reassure yourself that the thoughts and opinions of others do not matter and hilariously never have. Stupidly, you allowed it to have precedence in your life just for a little while and that short period of time was way too long. When you are forced out of your comfort zone and pressed to be wrinkle free, it is then when the steam of life makes your trials and tribulations crispy, no starch needed by the way. Things begin to work itself out without the extra things that are usually used to accomplish an expected result. Until we look in the mirror and take responsibility for our own actions then nothing will change, it ultimately starts with the individual self. It is easy to point the finger, but it is a task to hold yourself accountable. In times of

being on my lonesome, I tend to think about past events.
It is usually things that that has happened that made me
look at life in an inconceivable way. One day, me and my
brother walked over to Longwood, which was a store on
the southside of Chicago that was frequented by many.
On the way back, we were walking and came to the point
where we had to cross the train tracks. At the time I had a
hoodie over my head and headphones on. I did not know
that a Metra was currently approaching, and it was kind
of crazy because I heard my brother warn me through my
headphones. The Metra passed a few inches in front of
me swiftly and took my breath away. I removed the head
phones and looked back at my brother as he looked down
at the object he was holding in his hand and said, "OMG,
dang bro if you didn't stop me I would have gotten hit".
My brother replied, "I didn't say nothing, I thought that
you saw the train". I told him that I heard him tell me to
stop but he shook his head in an oblivious manner and
I knew that God had shielded me from what could have

been the end of my life. We must look back over our lives at times and if not to give thanks to God then to appreciate how far we have come. From at some points, times that we really thought about giving up. I worked the elections one year as an election judge and I had the honor of being graced by the presence of Oprah Winfrey while she came into the precinct to cast her vote. That moment did so much for me, it literally ignited a latent force inside of me that ensured me that I could overcome any circumstance, situation, etc. I had already started taking steps toward repairing the brokenness in my life but at that point I knew that I had to take full ownership. In front of me stood a woman of immeasurable high regard and although she was only human, she was one of the luminaries that exhibited true growth and evolution. More so, she had experienced some of the same things that I had in my child hood and her hapless story resonated with me in a manner that set the standard to persist and hang in there no matter what life throws at you. Seeing greatness in front of me ensured me that it was attainable. I just had

to put in the work to get there. My parents brought us up

in the church and although I use to hate going every time

the church doors were open, I'm so blessed to have been

introduced to Christ through the Church of God In Christ.

It really laid a firm foundation in my life to build upon,

no matter how many times I have been torn down, the

foundation has always been there to rebuild. Elder James

E. Young and Missionary Betty J. Young was an inspiration

to me growing up. Thinking about how certain people

contributed to me being who I am today overwhelms

me with joy. Uncle Jim and Aunt Jean was able to build a

church with very few members. Well, I can say it was a nice

number of members, but most of us were children. Our

family alone was enough to have a decent congregation.

Seeing the different stages that Love Community

C.O.G.I.C. went through definitely ensured me that God

can make a way out of no way. A lot of people doubted

Uncle Jim when he presented his vision of building a

million-dollar church with about ten adult members and over twenty kids. Despite the doubt dished his way, he kept the faith and was able to accomplish an extraordinary feat. Funding was procured and the new church that he promised was built. Seeing this, instilled in me the ability to keep pushing because your vision is not going to be understood by everyone but seeing the evidence of what no one else has, makes you know that you will come out on top. Sometimes, it is good to be on your "lonesome", when you can constructively examine your life and arrive at an indisputable conclusion, you have come to a destination that most do not reach.

Chapter 5:

The Breakdowns

O n many occasions, we tend to be shameful of our past and the things that we have experienced in our lives. The most important thing that someone can do concerning life's obstacles and roadblocks is to accept it and know that everything that you are faced with, you not only can but will overcome it. Everybody has moments in their lives where they are more weak than strong at times. The real problem is holding in so much instead of letting it all out. Holding in emotions, ill feelings and unresolved issues with others creates a toxic situation. Unknowingly,

you begin to become engulfed in a poisonous arena that

will eventually take over your mind, body, and soul, leaving

you to breakdown slowly. Personally, experiencing a

couple of breakdowns, the most difficult part is recovery.

Getting back to your normal self and what you feel

is comfortable and/or acceptable is extremely vital to restoring such a hideous mental state. Not sleeping, over analyzing things, uninvited burst of energy, etc. is just some of the things I experienced before having a breakdown. So, when things in life begin to make me feel that way, I just step back from everything. Realizing, that anything that makes me feel out of the ordinary is not worth it. I have always looked at my breakdowns as a revitalization because to rebuild something, you must first break it down. You always have a better chance at making things better when you already know where you went wrong before. It is great when you can become acquainted with a new and improved you. It is even greater when you have people around that love you and are there for you through the thick. To my TT whom I love so much, Angela Shaw, you do not know how much of watching your strength that enabled me to be strong myself. Your house was like my second home growing up and even though you fought a battle each day with having your only son taken from you,

you accepted me as your own. The love that you and Uncle Lou showed me throughout the years was a prescription filled that was not ordered by a doctor, but by God himself. You two provided me with peace and safety from things that had been going on that I thought that I could not talk about. I was with you two so much, that people would ask if me and Lil Lou were sisters when we went out in public. It is shocking how much we resembled each other. It was great to have such a wonderful friend/cousin and it was, LouSonja Shaw, "Lil Lou" as I would call her, along with others that helped me through my first break down. I am forever indebted to you all because you have always been a driving force in my life that will be there until God calls me home. That whole extended family was and still is the perfect painting of unwavering love through ups and downs. I am glad that I was able to take snippets of my life that enabled me to be the person that I am today. It is always wonderful to be able to share that of my own life experiences to help others. Always look at a breakdown as a good thing and if anybody tries to hold it against you it is only because they know that your future is brighter than theirs. The fear of someone passing them up, that they have referred to as "crazy", not only scares the hell out of them but it also makes them the equivalent or worse than what they have tried to label you as. My mom and dad once told me, while I was having a melt down after hearing the things that envious folks said about me, "Doesy, you have two degrees, you are very smart and intelligent, you're beautiful, you have been to the Army, you have a career and you taking good care of us. If you are crazy, then what does that make them?" That really made me think and I pulled myself together quickly. People will try to find the least relevant thing about you to make you feel less than. If you got it all together but you are obese, they are happy that they can say, you are fat. It is always something with people, that is the point that I am getting to. They may be broke, ugly, a hoe, on drugs, trying to come up with the next scam to finesse someone, not doing anything that will advance their life in a positive manner but they will find

the time to spread lies about you, and go even further by

talking about your few misfortunes. I always have found

it funny of how some people can mock your trials and

tribulations when those same obstacles could have been

avoided if they themselves were doing their part or helping

with something that should have been a group effort.

Everybody makes decisions and different choices in life

and unlike many I made the choice that I know was right.

While others chose the road common traveled, I chose

the road less traveled that constantly had construction

going on, leaving many detours. When you are a selfless

individual you tend to take the high road and you become

very familiar with the takers always taking and the givers

always getting taken advantage of. Stress is usually the

main source of breakdowns, but after reconnecting with

my biological family I found out some interesting facts

about my birth mother. She was brilliant with a wonderful

heart just like me but like many other individuals, she had

some underlying issues that took her away from reality at times. I accept my past; I am here in the present making the necessary adjustments for change and my future will not dictate what my history has once presented. I had rid myself of depression, it is no longer a part of me, but I was once very familiar with it.

Chapter 6:

Staying Positive Even If I Was Once Negative

It is extremely easy to be negative and I have never been an individual to accept a task that did not present a challenge. I always maintain a positive mind set no matter how much someone tries to bring me down. I realized that people would result to describing themselves when talking to others about you because if they do not know your business, believe me, they will make some up for

you. Why would or should I shed light on such a sorry

bunch of people? That would be like blaming the devil

for stuff that I know I like to do. I can honestly say that I

have always been a genuine and caring person, but I had to

learn the hard way that no matter what good you do some people will never be satisfied and a lot will even envy you. Back in elementary school I had not grasp this concept yet, so I found myself beating up some of my classmates and even including the teacher in some of the action. I had an extremely short temper and I really did not take no mess. When I say that I had zero tolerance for any type of annoyance, I literally mean zero tolerance. Back in my youth, I use to lay hands and contrary to what you may be thinking, it was far from holy. Fighting is how I dealt with my anger and although I would not pick on anyone, but I was not backing down on anybody trying to come at me. A lot of people from my old neighborhood are familiar with this portion of my life and may have even been the bag that landed some of my punches. Although I may have felt at the time that some deserved it, I apologize not only to you but publicly for beating on you. It was a phase in my life, but I have learned to control my anger and those that struggle with the same issue will hopefully get to this point one day as well. I remember throwing a chair at my fourth-grade teacher because she took my fruities. Now, for those of you that do not know what fruities are, it is a candy that is somewhat like a now and later, but better. It wasn't so much of the fact that she took my candy that prompted me to have the audacity to throw a chair at her, it was more so the nerve of her to take something away from me. I had already had so much taken away from me and mainly being deprived of not knowing who my biological family was and then she had the nerve to try to take away something that I held dear, my candy. At the time I had major anger issues and I am sure that many children faced with the mishap of being taken away from their families and placed somewhere else develops the same attributes that I once possessed. Back in elementary school I was a real riot and as I look back over my life and many events that transpired, I constantly ask myself....... how in the world did I make it this far? It was simply by the grace of God. I took my dad's gun from his lock box one day and ended up toting it to school, it was a 357 magnum, my most favorite weapon to this day but I ended up getting told on by one of my classmates. I really appreciate him for opening his mouth to speak up about something that should have never been done. Although at the time I thought it was all fun and games, he knew the danger of it, and I'm blessed to have witnessed such great character by one of my peers at an early age. When I found out that he had reported me I quickly hid it, and it was my word against his. I could have easily ruined my whole life from such a careless mistake. I never planned on using it, but I just thought that it was cool. It was not until I got grown that I realized how much of a blessing it was that God shielded me from what could have happened. When I reached the sixth grade that is when I began to try to change for the better. The first day of class as we all stood in the line outside of the classroom, waiting to go inside, I was pulled out of that line by my teacher. As the last student entered the classroom, my teacher slammed the door behind that student, and it was myself and Ms.

Freddie Thompson standing in the hallway face to face

and up personal. This woman conveyed a message to me

at that time that no one else had dared to do and she did

it with love while instilling some fear. She told me of how

she knew my family and was familiar with our story but

how I was not going to allow that to hinder me and how

I was basically going to get it together from that point on.

Wherever you are Ms. Thompson, I am elated to have

had you enter my life at the time you did. You made me

a better person! My attitude got better over time, but it

truly got better with understanding. Eventually you learn

that violence does not solve anything but silencing your

critiques through achievement is the sweetest revenge of all

time.

Chapter 7:

TAKERS & givers

In life, you have takers, and you have givers. Unfortunately, there are way more takers than there are givers. One thing that I had to realize is that when you give so often and to people that are so underserving of your gifts that things can get "real" very quickly. Some people tend to act as if it is expected and that you must do things for them, they get a feeling of entitlement. I found myself in a situation whereas when I finally got around to learning to say the word "no", some people acted as if I was doing an injustice to them. It was hilarious to say the least, especially seeing that these same people would never be there for me if I needed them. I had to get to a mindset that if I did not help that individual then what would they do? It is simple. They would go ask the next person, but because they knew that I would always say "yes", I was often the first target. It kind of puts you in the position to act outside of yourself to not get taken advantage of. I have always been a genuine giver, so to have to adjust the way you are to maintain yourself and not so much as others, it is a pretty difficult task. The urban dictionary tends to have some pretty good explanations of words that cannot be defined thoroughly with other dictionaries; with takers and givers being two of them. The urban dictionary describes takers as someone who always takes from other people and never gives back and it defines givers as someone who will do anything for anyone. When you do so much for certain individuals, they get so inclined to your giving and their taking that when you begin to give to someone outside of them, they get jealous. Everything happens when God sees fit. I noticed a high change in my life when I started to pray differently. I have always felt like a senior citizen in a young person's body. I asked God to please provide me with the necessities of life and if He saw fit to add some accessories then as long as His will was done, I was fine with that. Now, I know some of you don't have a belief in God and that's your choice but I have been placed in situations and have grown through certain things that I know that the Lord God is real. If it was not for him and other people in my life telling me to focus on myself and my child, then I would still be doing things for people that literally meant me no good. You must learn to first and foremost, make sure that you are good. Some people will try to count your money even though it is certainly not helping them make any and will assume that you have things that has never been in your sight. I have given my last to people that were nothing, but takers and I knew that but more importantly, God knew my heart. Some people think that you are unaware of their deceitfulness. When, you really have been playing chess while they are still trying to grasp the concept of checkers. Doing a good person wrong that would go out of their way to help only makes you lose someone that is a blessing to have. There is no one on this Earth that is comprised the way that you are. You are not one in a million, but we are all one in a lifetime. I heard Bishop T.D. Jakes once say, "some people just hate you because you're blessed." That had been the story of my life and I felt every bit of his words. Well, hater hate on! I have already adopted Jill Scott's "Hate on Me" as my theme song, but I will no longer be a GIVER to any takers. Takers cannot be helped, not by you anyway. They tend to express a love for money and material things that truly overtakes them. We live in a day and age where people will go as far as befriending you just to try to get over on you. It comes a time in life to express facts and to not include any emotions and when that is done, and things are still not understood than the next step is to let go. You cannot fault anyone but yourself when you have created such an environment to be taken advantage of, but you can fault others when they

cannot accept the gist of you moving on.

Chapter 8:

All Over The Place

I thought to myself, what chapter should this information go in? I already warned you all that I would bounce around a lot in trying to portray my life. Well, in this chapter even more so. Let us just get started! My biological family found me back in 2010 while I was going through Postpartum Psychosis which is when a woman experiences a break from reality after giving birth to a child. You may not be familiar with this medical term but going through this situation/obstacle made me dive into research on it after God had given me the ability to be blessed to be back

Closed File Information and Search Service

a program of the
Illinois Department of Children and Family Services

delivered by
Midwest Adoption Center

Reply to:
Deanna P.
3158 South River Road Suite 224
Des Plaines, IL 60018
Phone: 847/298-9096 x23
Email: DeannaP@macadopt.org

March 18, 2010

Jasmine Jones

Dear Ms. Jones:

I am writing to you about a very personal matter. You may be an important person in the life of someone who is seeking to locate birth relatives. While this information may come as a surprise to you, please let me explain the circumstances under which I am contacting you.

The Illinois Department of Children and Family Services now offers a variety of services to anyone who was placed in adoption through DCFS, was in foster care through DCFS or who is related to such a person. I am a caseworker at Midwest Adoption Center, an agency that provides some of those services for the Department. I have enclosed a description of the program that this agency has been providing for DCFS since 1993.

DCFS records provided to us indicate that you are the younger birth sister of a person born in April 1974. Your relative has asked the Department to contact you on her behalf.

Your birth sister would like to know how you are doing, and wants to share information with you about her life. She stated that you have two brothers, and that she would also like to provide some information about your birth mother. Your birth sister is interested in being in contact with you.

If you believe that you are NOT related to this person, it is important that you tell me so that I can continue trying to locate the correct person. IDCFS records and information about the persons involved is kept strictly confidential. At no time will I or this agency release any information about you to any other party without your consent to do so.

If you are the correct person, you have several options.

> 1. *If both you and your birth relative agree, you can exchange medical or other information, letters or photographs without revealing your name or location. I would be glad to explain more about how you can communicate anonymously. It may be very helpful to you and to your birth relative to share information even if you do not have any direct contact. After exchanging letters and/or information, you can decide whether to end the communication or to release your name and contact information to the birth relative.*

Midwest Adoption Center

3158 South River Road – Suite 224   Phone: 847-298-9096   MAC@macadopt.org
Des Plaines, Illinois 60018   FAX: 847-298-9097   www.macadopt.org

---

in my right mind. I discussed earlier in the book that my biological mom would default from reality at times and that is because she had a bipolar disorder. A family history of this is considered a significant risk factor for postpartum psychosis. It was during this time that I came to a huge understanding that you CAN NOT control what happens within your body. I experienced a hideous mental state, it was as if I was present in my body, but I had no control over what I was saying or doing. Like a charley horse, it came and went as it wanted. I was dehydrated and my body had started to respond. It was not water that I needed but HELP with all the responsibility that had been placed on me. Life became even more overwhelming, with the addition of bringing a beautiful baby girl in the world. I was never an individual that would swear, but during that time of my life I became a cursing sailor. The truth of the matter is, we all go through stuff and most people try to hide their low times as if they are just so unscarred. I remember telling my mom that raised me before going through this that, "God is not real, if he was then I wouldn't have been given up or I wouldn't be going through the things that I was faced with." My mom replied, "Doesy, God will show you that He is real. Mark my words…". Sure enough, God showed me that He is real over all things. While going through Postpartum Psychosis, not only did my mother pray me out of that situation but I promised God that if he brought me out of such a horrendous mental state that I would never question His existence again. I was able to fully recover from that situation due to God reuniting me with my biological family. Many of the questions I had growing up were answered. I also found out that my parents never gave me up but that I had been taken by DCFS because of a situation with my birth mother. All efforts were made to get me back, but I was still misplaced. I call this organization/system hideous because, instead of trying to make sure that children remain with their biological families, they would rather place them with strangers who one too many times provide a life much worse than that of the one they would have had with their birth parents. I was able to reconnect with my family on my biological mother, Diane Head-Adams, side and to see where I got my smarts and golden heart from was gratifying. My biological family is amazing and even though I still have a lot to connect with, I am sure God will provide me with the life health and strength to do so. I learned that my mother had four children with me being the baby. Angelia Head (R.I.P.), Terrence Adams, Johnny Williams, Jr., and Angelina Denise Williams (myself). It did not stop there because my father, Johnny Lee Williams, Sr., provided me with an overload of family to be embraced by. I get excited every time I think about his mother, my grandmother Corrine Williams, and how good of a cook she is. From the first time I met her it was as if I had been around her my whole life. Nobody makes a better butter roll then her and I will bet my last on that! Just when I thought that life could not get any more satisfying, my dad introduced me to big my sister Tiffany Taylor-Percy. Ever since my family found me, she has been rocking and I have been rolling. She helped me get to the point that I could not only just be me, but she provides me with a since of security. She is the protector that I have always been with

my adoptive family and it is great to see where some of
my traits come from. She would not care for me to list her
accomplishment and what she had to go through to get
there but she has an extraordinary story that helped me
out. I am overwhelmed with emotions from the blessings
that God has bestowed on my life. I have a lot of family
with big titles and I can rant and rave about that, but the
truth of the matter is that titles mean nothing. Also, while
a degree is an extraordinary piece of paper to possess
only because education was not afforded to some of us
at one point; those things do not make or break you. If
you do not have the wisdom and knowledge to use your
mouthpiece to speak up and get what you want, then all
that stuff is just in vain. My parents that raised me only had
a third-grade education and they accomplished way more
than people with doctorates. My aunt Caroline Hughes
and her husband, Uncle Mike, gave me background and
information on my biological mom side recently that really
touch me. I am glad that it has been a group effort with

making me aware and showing that I come from a loving

family. My aunt Willie Bell from out west had given me

the best and most detailed biography of my birth mom.

I realized that the way people perceive you is from that

of their life experiences with you. Just like when I have

moved to a new area, people unfamiliar with me before

would think that I was an angel, not knowing that I had

just stepped out of hell. A niece, from my adoptive family,

tried to contact my biological sister through Facebook and

had the nerve to try to slander my name. It was hurtful

when my sister told me about this, seeing that I had done

so much for this individual. She was just showing who not

only herself, but who some members of her immediate

family had always been. Thanks sweetheart, it just brought

me and my sister/biological family closer together! I know

you would probably like me to go more into depth with

reuniting with my biological family, but I must stay on task

with the point I am trying to make in this book. You can

weather any storm and even when you think that you have

reached the end of the line, God will throw you some more rope. Just, keep on keeping on!

Chapter 9:

The Prayer Warrior

My mother that raised us was a devout Christian and an even better prayer warrior. I can remember hearing prayers flowing through the halls and stairwells of our house at the wee hours of the morning. Although I never understood why she prayed so much as well as placed blessed oil on every last one of our bodies, eventually I came to the realization that she had been shielding us all from hurt, harm and danger throughout the years. They say that the prayers of the righteous availeth much and Mrs. Jones was as righteous as they

came. Her prayers were so astounding and pure, not because she was so good at praying but because she lived a life that was beholding to the beliefs that she portrayed to others. Mama was a phenomenal woman and the greatest role model any child or adult could look up to. She made her mark in this world. Her DASH (-) meant something!

My adopted mother was always a true example of what
a Christian should be. There is no sugar coating her
amazing attributes that allowed me to see the true glory
of God. She legally adopted nine children and had been
a foster mother to a countless number of children. It was
her prayers and selfless service that kept several biological
families together and by God's grace she and my dad were
able to raise us all quite well. I'm sitting here typing and
as I'm reminiscing on those days, I can hear my mother
walking through the house each and every night singing
"Just another day that the Lord has kept me, he has kept me
from all evil, with a mind stayed on him, just another day
that the Lord has kept me." The anointing that was in this
woman was so real that not even the devil could deny that
she was touched and blessed by the best. When Lillie Mae
woke up in the morning and went to sleep at night, every
unkempt spirit felt her presence and knew that they would
have to answer to a higher being one day and in our house,
we served the Lord. God was truly good to us throughout

the years and his grace and mercy was bountiful. We were always two flowers growing in the rain and blooming in the sun (Lillie & Jasmine). If love would have kept her here, she would have never left this earth. Lillie, you were my everything and if I do not know anything else, I know that I took good care of my mother. Some people are so quick to say, "I know how you feel" or "I feel your pain". Please, just shut up! Because you do not, your relationship with your love ones may be completely different than that of mine. Everybody does not love their parents, siblings, family in general the same. Some folks can care less about a person's well-being or how they are faring in life. When your love and genuine care matches that of mine for the love ones I lost, then and only then can you say that. Until then, keep on living. My mother had a mouth like a sword, if you thought that you were going to try her, try again. She could put together an array of words that would make you rethink your whole life's existence. The shocking thing about it was that she did not have to curse to get her point across. Our dad was more laid-back and mainly stayed in the living room watching cartoons most of the day. Do not get it twisted though, if you for once thought that you were about to disrespect Lillie Mae, that is when you would be hearing from my dad. The way my dad protected my mom was amazing and vice versa. He never allowed anyone to utter a negative word about my mom. They stuck together, no matter what. I just hope to have one third of that type of love one day. My mother will always be the love of my life and in that alone she can rest up. She did an exceptional job on this earth and touched many lives in ways that most would view as impossible. I am at peace knowing that she is finally in peace. I showed her that I loved her each day, and she left this world knowing just that. It has been several years since God called her home and I cannot think of a better deserving child of God. I cannot thank her enough for instilling in me strength, genuine love, her praying abilities, and a countless number of other attributes that I could not have obtained from anywhere else. Until we meet again as she would always say, "Doesy Woesy, you know I love you den doe!" Well, you know I love you more mama!

Chapter 10:

Even Gold Gets Tarnished

"Our daddy sometimes kept to himself. Chose his words wisely and rarely opened-up. But when he did speak, you listened. He showed his love through providing and maintaining a household, maintaining a family. He showed me that you do not have to talk about it to BE about it. A father is a verb. It is the things you did that made you Pops. You made me a stand-up Man."

~Vincent Maurice Jones

My dad always taught me that a man would rather be

respected than loved. A wedding lasts a day and a marriage

last a lifetime. I will invest in the bigger picture any day. I hate you is thrown around a lot. A lot of times people only mean, I love you, but I hate the things you do. Also, what you allow is what will continue. You come to realize a lot dealing with various situations and people. It is like dating outside of your race because everyone can not relate. A lot of times I found myself misunderstood, but not everyone has the same level of understanding or intellect as yourself so it may be hard for them to comprehend you. You still must be yourself, unique and genuine in all things and eventually you will be surrounded by like-minded people. Individuals that do not share your same opinions, but people who do not mind you having your own. I cannot thank my dad enough for everything that he taught me and the wisdom that he instilled in me. My father would always kneel alongside his bed and say a prayer in silence. He was consistent with this, every morning after waking up and at night before going to bed. I never knew exactly what he prayed about but through that I saw his relationship with the Lord God. Which is the only thing that mattered.

One of his best attributes was minding his own business. My father gave me a business mindset. He would tell us about how his grandfather, T.J. Huddleston, Sr., founded the first black hospital in Mississippi. T.J. was his mother's, Blanche Huddleston, father. Growing up, my parents would bring us back to their hometowns in Mississippi and being city kids raised on the south side of Chicago, we could understand why they left. Seeing my father first cousin fight for a better Mississippi has been one of the best parts of moving down to the magnolia state. My dad used to take us over to his uncle's rib joint off Stoney Island in Chicago, best known as Leon's BBQ and we use to be able to get whatever we wanted. When it came to traveling, I gained so many frequent driver miles. This was because if it was not a car, preferably a Cadillac, daddy was not getting in it. I enjoyed driving my parents all over the U.S. and watching them enjoy life in their well-seasoned years. Now, I ride around in my deceased Pops car because it is near to me, dear to me, it is mine you see. Hate me, love me, or have no concern but I loved my father and mother unconditionally and I know most people do not experience that type of love. Without my father, our mother would have not been able to get us. My family has gone through a true healing stage of trying to deal with our issues, disagreements, major hurt as well as disappointment but I know that if we stick together, we will all overcome. I cried while writing this chapter because my heart was crushed seeing my sister, whom I once thought to be my mother growing up, hurt throughout the years and trying to cope with something that society has thrown under the rug for so long. That same rug has been walked over and not cared for one bit. If this book does nothing more than to help the young women and men of all ages deal with the devastation of being molested or verbally abused, then I have done my due diligence. I too was molested growing up, but it was not by my father. It hurt me deeply when I had my first child, after being told by doctors that I would probably not be able to have children, that rumors spread that I was pregnant by my father. I know some of

my siblings voiced concerns because they care for me and

genuinely love me but for others that had spent my whole

life being envious and jealous of God placing me in my

adoptive parents' life was another thing. I do not have to

say names or go into detail because when you know the

things that you have done to someone that was wrong,

your conscious tends to eat away at you. Looking around, I

see the effects, but I certainly will not say that I am happy

that you have not amounted to anything except a constant

reminder of what I never want to be. You are either reading

this dreading the next thing that I may say or ready for

some real tea, but I will not give that satisfaction. At least

not in this book anyway. Let me be clear, my father had

never done anything to me or even looked at me wrong.

This does not excuse anything that may have happened

to others. Personally, I will not even shed light on those

that abused me because it is already dim where they are in

life right now. I chose to give it to God and trust me, He

has handled them quite well. Everybody is different but I challenge you to do the same after taking whatever avenues necessary to assist in stopping this horrific issue. It was not until my later and more informed years that I realized how much disfunction went on in my life growing up. Has anyone not lived in a household that played "house" as kids? I was sick also and although those that played along was around the same age, things manifested in me that had been done to me by others that knew better and were grown adults. I thought that was okay and when I got older, I began to go into deep thought about it and ended up having a break down. I apologized to different individuals and surprisingly they said that they knew what they were doing, and no apology was needed. It was good to get that off my conscious and when I asked for forgiveness the same grace and mercy that I had given to others was granted to me. For those people that may have placed me on a pedestal and thought that some type of perfection existed, it does but in the form of truth and accepting that

I am flawed like anyone else. So, even what you may have thought was gold and what I may have thought was gold, has officially been tarnished! We all need to learn how to go and seek help, nobody on God's creation is perfect. Stop running around talking about others when your thoughts and wrong doings are the equivalent of any prisoner doing a life sentence. Your truth has not been spoken yet and it is hiding in something much more fragile than a closet, it is in your mind. Crap happens and it is up to you to clean it up or dwell in it. You choose!

Chapter 11:

Heaven Sent

G rowing up there were many people that came in and out of my life that was a major influence on who I am today; some positive and some negative but these people are nonetheless truly significant to me. There are a few individuals that really helped me along the way and what better way to pay them back than to add a chapter in my first book to personally thank them. I am definitely not about to mention every person and if you thought that you had done so much in my life that you should be mentioned than if not now, maybe at a later time. Two of the pillars of

Myself, Dave Green and Laverne Green

the Morgan Park community, Dave, and Laverne Green,

were always a beautiful couple from our neighborhood that

dedicated their lives to helping others. Not only that, but

Dave was and will always be the Original "Chicago Piano

Man". It was these two that planted the seed of selfless service in me and from there a beautiful crop has grown.

They allowed me to be a part of their lives in a way that ministered healing to my soul. Mrs. Green would teach us about the Lord God and being born again. This amazing woman would make things so simple that anyone could understand how easy it is to make it into Heaven. God knows your heart and your mind so He can take it from there. Mr. and Mrs. Green would find all types of things around the house for us to do and honestly that was one of the best jobs that me and some of my siblings had. They kept funds in our pocket that helped us get clothes that did not come from the Salvation Army or Good Will. Me and my brother were able to hit up Evergreen Plaza to get us some fresh gear. They would take us on projects with them and one I remember so well. We went to the house of a couple that needed help clearing things out. When we all arrived, me and the kids that had come along to assist were blown away to learn the true definition of hoarders. We all learned a lot working on that project and came to know some wonderful people. Those that were there can attest to this story and I am sure it will stay in the most memorable memories for each one of us. We helped that couple restore the cleanliness of their home that they had allowed to completely get away from them with junk and clutter. This is true in a lot of our lives, but guess what? You can be restored also. Mrs. Green use to also teach us these things in the bible lessons that I had the pleasure of being a part of at their "south side mansion" as Mr. Green would put it. May God rest his extraordinary soul, as my Uncle Jim (Elder James E. Young) use to say, as he "left the land of the dying and entered into the land of the living" on February 4, 2019.

Mrs. Green can still be found on the south side of Chicago being a breath of fresh air and a beam of sunshine. Some people think that because you have gone through something that you are entitled to sympathy and special treatment but that is certainly false. Being adopted or being a foster child does not mean that you are entitled to things because the life that you have been given. It means just the opposite and that is that you have to work twice as hard if you want to be successful and the most effective way is to be around people that can enable you to reach your goals. The most important thing that I learned from Dave and Laverne is that it's not what you do for others, it's the approach you take and the genuine nature that it is coming from. A lot of people do things to be seen and to get some type of recognition for it. Think what you want, but I have my own opinion and I do not like that type of mentality or attitude. It is not becoming, and I feel that it is what is wrong with society today. If you can help someone, please just do it without having to broadcast it. Dave and Laverne were a true reflection of that throughout the years, most people would not believe the things they did for others. I was able to absorb that from them and I notice that I forget good deeds done because it was God that used me to reach that individual, it was never my doing. If God is a part of it then it will be a blessing to others and if you keep at it, it

could be a blessing to you as well.

Chapter 12:

Chosen

It is imperative that you understand the greater good of being given up and taken in. A lot of times we focus solely on the negative aspects instead of embracing the positive. There comes a time in life where you must realize your worth and the fact that most people do not have enough value to even afford your company. One of the most hilarious memories that I can recall is my first time going to a club/lounge. I was never able to rap my mind around the idea of paying to get into a place to dance and drink. I always thought that for one, I cannot

really dance so dancing at home for free was a much better

idea. Secondly, I did not drink and quite frankly I do

not like being around that type of environment because

I had seen so much happen in the presence of alcohol.

Just like any other drug, it takes an individual away from

their originality and makes them someone outside of

themselves. Somewhat like wearing make-up, it hides

your true self because there is no purity in it. Anyway, I

walk into this lounge/club in full church attire, I'm talking

Church of God In Christ, could pass for Easter Sunday in a

Baptist Church type of outfit and I knew that I had dressed wrong when the music stopped as I entered the door. My best friend told me quickly to take the church hat off. We went into the rest room to correct this unfortunate mishap, but I realized that I had not been missing out on anything by staying away from the club/lounge. I concluded that certain things are not for everybody and some of us have callings on our lives that obligates us to get to a point where we know without a shadow of doubt that we are handpicked. I can remember every person that has ever told me that I would never amount to anything, that I was a foster child and that my biological parents did not want me. I even remember some people saying that my parents were crack heads, and the list goes on. Do not ever to listen to such ignoble and foul individuals. Some will say that this is airing your dirty laundry. I will just say that I am finally getting around to washing my clothes. It is a process that you go through when you have been through things, like clothes. When your clothes get dirty, you will either wash them right away, not most people. Or, put them in a basket and let them pile up. When you let them pile up, the likelihood of being able to get out stains becomes less likely. This goes for that of our own lives as well. Start cleaning up mess right away, do not wait until it gets so bad that you feel as if you have thrown your life away. When I began to accept the fact that when you are a foster child or adopted that you are literally chosen; life became more meaningful. Parents that birthed their own children did not have a choice of whether that child was going to be a girl or boy, they couldn't decide that they wanted to skip the baby years and get straight to adolescents more so that their child would smart or not so bright. Some children were even aborted before having the chance to experience life, but it has been a favor for us all to grace this Earth. Being chosen on the other hand, parents get you pretty much on a trial basis during foster care and if your biological parents aren't able to get you back because of life circumstance then those parents can possibly choose to adopt you. They have been given the well needed time to see how smart you are, they already know whether you are a girl or a boy and most importantly they have discerned that they would like you to be a part of their lives for the rest of your life. Parents seem to be the only ones obligated to love you; from the rest of the world you must earn it. Choose to consider yourself CHOSEN.

Chapter 13:

Depression

Sometimes the pains of life outweigh the will to live. You just have to realize that not every day will be a good day and that life consist of many ups and downs, it's what you do in the midst of those things that will determine the outcome of bigger and better things for your life. I had to conclude that in every negative aspect of life that if I embraced the positive then things would be alright for me. After losing my mother I received several phone calls from bill collectors trying to reach her and I notified them that she had passed and all they could do is write things off as a loss but while she lived I'm sure they stressed her out. I wondered if I died today what would happen? Nothing. Life would go on and the world would keep revolving. So, why is it that I worry about things that I cannot change? It was then that I realized that being depressed over things was no longer an option for me. If something did not make me better, contribute to my well-being and happiness then I did not want to have any part of it because it was simply toxic. Sometimes in life a person cannot explain why they act in the way they act. Most times they are acting in a way that they feel is suitable for the situation from experiences in that of their own life. Love makes you feel like you can do more in life but feeling as if you are not loved back makes you destructible. Everything happens when God sees fit. I noticed a change in my life when I started to pray differently. I have always felt like a senior citizen in a young person body, so my generation was completely unlike me. I asked God to please provide me with the necessities and if He saw fit to add some accessories then as long as His will was done

that, I would be alright. Now I know some of you don't

have a belief in God and that's your choice, but I have

been placed in situations and have gone through certain

things that I know that the Lord God is real. I missed so

many days of school growing up, but I still was able to

graduate with honors. So, make no excuse, where there

is a will, there is certainly a way. I had to take care of my

parents who had fallen ill and honestly, that was rough. It

weighed on me so much that it became the main source

of my depression. I could not wrap my mind around how

my parents had raised many children and how my mom

had dedicated her life to being there for others but in her

time of need, I could hear crickets. My father did not care

who came around and was not too fond of many people

anyway. My mother desired to be surrounded by those

that she loved the most though. It hurt me seeing my mom

hurt because she did not deserve the way she was treated at

the end of her life. She did all she could for everybody and even if some of you may not have thought it was the best, she did her best! There are things that my mom discussed that I will not mention to preserve the hearts and minds of some people that know they did not do their part. If your parents are still breathing, I appeal to you to try your best to appreciate them as much as possible. All of us do not have the best of parents, but if they are still present in our lives then trying to mend whatever issues you have with them is important. You never want to regret not doing what you know you should have done. For all the people out there taking care of your parents alone, keep up the great work. It is tiring, demanding and you must deal with their denials of growing old and them sometimes being ornery because of that. Thinking about how you have other siblings that have gone on to live their life not keeping in mind that the ones that have raised them are aging, is something I had to accept. I had to utilize that energy to focus on my purpose and if my parents would have never adopted me, who would have taken care of them? Chills go through my body thinking of this. I know that I have been the joke of some conversations because I almost lost my mind taking care of my parents. Weak minded people will always try to talk about your lows in life when they feel that you are outshining them. No need to front your move or act like you have been there when you know you have not. The good thing is that life goes on and you still have a chance to change for the better. My mother always told me, "Doesy, don't worry.... when these hands get cold, they are going to wish that they had done right by me den doe. God gone bless you for taking care of me and Junior. You have always been a good child and we have loved you since we got you. You are going to have it all one day, so much that you won't know what to do with it but me and Junior won't be here to see it". No matter how much you love your family and want to see everyone do well, they may not feel the same way for whatever reasons they have been feeding themselves. Letting go of toxic things and toxic people is the best cure for any type of depression. It is the only cure.

No medicine ever created can accomplish what the power

of "Letting go and letting God" could do.

Chapter 14:

Scapegoat

Sometimes you may experience times in life where you feel that you are up against everything. During these times is where I began to grow a fond interest in sports, poetry and helping others. In elementary school, I was always getting suspended or had in school suspension from distasteful behavior. I loved it because I could do stuff that challenged me and held my attention for what they thought was punishment. The in-school suspension teacher provided me the well needed one on one attention that I so desperately yearned for and I was able to just put certain things into perspective that I didn't quite understand at the time. It was hard being at home all day with a house full of kids and then coming to school to a classroom full of them. Although my behavior was not the best, I always excelled academically scoring at extremely high levels on the Iowa Test of Basic Skills (ITBS) to pass on to the next grade. Sometimes you must play the dummy to expose the fool. Even though I hated to move from the city in high school, it was necessary. When my parents moved us out to the suburbs in efforts to get us away from all the violence that was happening on the south side of Chicago, it was like a culture shock. Our first day in Park Forest was spent at the basketball courts doing what we did best, and we came across some wonderful souls that summer. Now when school started, that was another story. We were new but because our parents were older and not in the best of health, staying out of trouble was our focus. A lot of the kids at the school we attended did not even know how the situation that I was faced with saved them from getting their heads knocked off. Yes, some of the little suburbanites thought that they were tough and although they needed to see the "Doesy" side of me, I only showed Jasmine. You must see the bigger picture though and the fact of the matter was that I had been given a fresh start. I had to embrace it and continue to progress from my old ways. This was a true escape. It was so different form the city, they had all types of stuff in the suburban schools like "The Gay/Straight Alliance" and "Thespians". We did not know what all that was at the time. Meanwhile, where we came from, they had "Staying in the Closet" and if you could act, "Get There on Your Own". Why was this stuff not accessible to many of the city kids? A lot of people would have done better in life being acquainted with individuals that were free to be themselves. Where I grew up at, those things were kind of frowned upon. I am "strictly dickly", although I have experimented like many of you all. Anyway, I love everybody, but I know some people that those student body organizations could have helped.

During this time was when the biggest changes took place in my life. I wanted to share a few of my poems, these poems represent the different mental states I was once in. From depression, breakdowns, feeling loved and even motivated through enlightenment these poems were my scapegoat.

Personage

Perplexed, but her inner thoughts glow

Relished I life's unbeatable sociopolitical flow

Staring at the infinite line of instant measures aimed at
cutting back on our own displeasures

Fed up with constantly being befuddled about the next
generations struggles

Men-folk step aside, time for the sisterhood to take a ride

Brutality is harsh, but what's worst is the unspoken words of
mysterious force trapped behind barriers and multitudes of
unforgettable distrust

Speak! Let the world hear your voice

Remembering the pas and striving for our obscure future,
where dreams prevail because of the obsession of the
obligation to start unfamiliar cases

Boycotted so that we stood out from all races

Now having respect because Rosa did something morally outrageous

Igniting the uproar of a peculiar nation

Parks led from the front so recognize her innovation

Laid to rest but not forgotten

Paved the way by starting a mission

Stand up proud and stand up free

Traveling any and everywhere in the front

Because Rosa Parks made a difference for you and me!

Candid Love

All those other dudes were my lesson, and you are my

Heaven-sent blessing

Extraordinary in every way, it is funny how everything about

you leaves me in a daze

My mental state for you is too complicated to explain

The evidence of pleasure cannot differentiate to distant

measures

Your cordiality is so rare that to no man do you compare

It is explicit to me that you will always be near

My necessity to love is benevolent to few, I would rather not

say it for those that show it are more true

Ecstasy is a meaningless term but when I am trying to

describe the words for you, I yearn

Grapes condensed to wine saturates my essence of being

intertwined

Discrimination is not my trade so discreet is where disclosure

shall take its place

You convey to me attributes of a sensual source, that with

time and patience resemblance or originality will run its

course.

Denial

Tight chest, frustrating thoughts, locked up behind my own pitfalls of mishaps

Me against myself, did my heart just stop?

I am in a whirlwind of denial, but I cannot accept it

So, I am trying, steady stuck, trying to figure my own self out

So much anger, pain.

I am missing out on fear

Stop, think, learn what? To be wise, try foolish

Is life a joke? Wait a minute, am I talking about denial or am I just so mixed up that my mind is in a front? I am what I am, I am not what you are or want

I am in denial of myself

I existed in past, I exist in the present, but I do not want to be presents past future

I want to be the pasts future present

I am in denial that I was born to fail

I have always had an unrealistic future

Dreams do not come true, especially when you have failed to prescribe the task at hand

What am I talking about?

I have no idea, but the worldly name for it is confusion, no I have gone crazy

Humanity cannot even cure me now

Drugs have already been tried against my will and it is tearing me up inside

I am unfit for society; I am the joke?

Gone head state your quote

Thrown away at birth like a dirty rag torn from mold

Who am I? Where am I? Why am I? Answer me.

Wait, am I going into another panic attack?

I hate life, or does life hate me?

Am I in denial of little or big things?

Can I be reborn, so I can swipe my past and present away, to escape this hideous mental state

Something wants my mind, and I am tired of fighting for it everyday

What is it? Who is it? Why is it?

Am I in denial that several years has passed since I have begged God to take me away?

From what? Misery, wrong-doing, cold-heartedness

An overly intelligent mind given at birth

A wise intelligent mind progressed

Kept from the foolish mind of death

Denial

Denial

Denial

Denial

I am my own DENIAL!!!!!!

TIRED

Thoughts of being unknown is simple when

Irresponsible is life's thrown, it is true that

Rejection is the quick way out, while

Excuses is replaced with worry and doubt and

Denial is the main thing we read and hear about

TIRED!!!!

Imagine Me

It is clear that my success line is irrelevant

Standing in my way, I doubt I will put up with it

Imagine me or Imagine you?

I would rather Imagine myself doing what I must do

Firefighter, Policeman, Lawyer or Pediatrician

Whatever you put your mind to you can beat any intuition

My ambitions are so high that I envy the people that try me

I just recollect the damage and throw out the things behind me

Imagine me, being what I want to be

A successful black strong woman in a world full of misery

I thank God that failure has never been a part of me

In fact, proving many wrong has been a lesson without a key

I try to be, society's outcast of statistics because it is not of me

Whether you Imagine me, or I Imagine myself

I am going to do what I Imagine of me

A beautiful being striving to be what I want to be

So just, IMAGINE ME.

The Storm

I was blessed with a vocabulary so strong

That I can go off the top of my dome and simply befuddle you

I plan to eradicate the norms because I am different, authentic.

Can you see this storm that is headed your way?

They call it a Category 5 and Hurricane Jas requires you to evacuate.

Please do not take my kindness for weakness.

I can be the child of God that I was born to be or the Devil's Advocate that you surely do not want to see.

As you can tell? I am angry.

You should be alarmed because after this storm the flood will drown you.

Now you waiting to be aided as I abated

but you were warned before I made it

So, may God bless you.

Chapter 15:

The Turning Point

My mother use to always tell me that "you can run but you can't hide". She always felt that I had a calling on my life and that if I did not live right then things would not go right for me. I always had my mother father, sister, etc. to talk to about things that bothered me or even things that I needed closure on, and they were able to help me out a great deal. My sister ended up dying on March 9, 2014 followed by my mother on November 23, 2014 and my dad on January 2, 2016. I experienced so many other losses during that span of time and certainly after. I went

through a period of deep depression and really feeling like

I had no one to talk to or turn to for help. It was then that

I realized that the Lord God was showing me that I no longer had options and that my help came from Him and only Him. It was at this point that I had to rely on God because man will fail you. This was the turning point of my life. I had literally dedicated my life to taking care of my parents and helping others that I was kind of lost when I no longer had them physically present with me.

After praying and seeking God to direct my path. I decided to move from Chicago on a Friday and me as well as my daughter was on the road by that Wednesday. I packed all my things myself and got the largest U-Haul truck available with an auto transport. I moved most of the things out of my home with minor assistance from some neighbors. I even put some Jehovah Witnesses to work while they were ministering in the neighborhood. I would not have been able to get those couches out without them. I stepped out on faith and with the surety that God would not only provide my needs but some of my wants also. I say all this to say, you do not need anybody or anything, but God and he will give you the strength to move forward. If you are willing then believe me, He is able. I moved down to the coast of Mississippi in 2017, Gulfport to be exact. I have been able to forge many wonderful friendships with some great people. I owe the Coast for helping me come out of a darkness that had almost claimed my life. I was a ticking time bomb and while a few people saw it, a lot of people down here unknowingly helped me out. The Coast is serenity in the time of trouble and good cheer when you need it the most. I have never been around folks that are crazy enough to speak to strangers as if they had known them their whole life. I guess I have gotten an overdose of what you all call southern hospitality. Coming from Chicago you must be cognizant of things like that. I felt like somebody was trying to set me up, but that was just a notion from being a product of the environment in which I grew up in.

When you reach the point in your life where you accept yourself and I'm referring to the adequate, substandard and undisclosed parts; it is then and only then when you

are able to take complete hold of your life and to just allow

the Lord God to truly move. I used to hear all the time

at church that you should speak things as if they were.

I can admit that I use to take that statement way too far

growing up but the hilarious part about it is that some of

those things manifested in my life. It was simply a lie told

at the time, on myself though. As my Pawpaw (Green D.

Ingram) use to say, "I lied", when asked about false things

that he once spoke of in the past. At least I was not running

around lying on other people like some of you all do on a

regular basis. If I said something about somebody else, it

was certainly a fact; no fiction about it. I must say that I

have grown into an individual that no longer defaults from

the truth. Accept me or not, but I am done with lying. I

was still a minor back then and going through so much

in life mentally, emotionally, and spiritually; it caused me

to present a representative of myself like a lot of people

do because the fear of not being liked or accepted for

being themselves. By the way, if you have ever lied at least once, that would make you a liar. Folks will always have something to say and the better you do fortunately the more their mouths will yap about you. I say fortunately because you have got to be an exceptional individual when you are on the minds and tongues of people that do not even cross your thoughts. All lies told on me does not even have to be addressed because the truth will always prevail. In this "Turning Point" of my life, I choose to move forward. So, if you ever thought that you truly knew me; that was then, this is now and let us just call it a turning point. Forgetting and forgiving those that have done me wrong and asking for forgiveness from those that I may have wronged. For those that have tried to cause true misfortune in my life, I must get something off my chest. Your shame is in knowing what you did as well as said and the fact that you will have to live with such guilt for the rest of your life. You may have thought that you had broken me, but you only made me stronger. So, kudos, you have finally gained your applause. As I stated in my introduction,

I have always desired to aspire to be and do whatever I

wanted; even as an adolescent I had big dreams. Contrary

to your popular demand and beliefs, I will continue to

prosper and not a devil from Hell will stop me! Gratitude.

About the Author

Jasmine Jones was born and raised in Chicago, Illinois. She was adopted by Lonnie Jones, Jr. and Lillie Mae Jones. Jasmine was brought up in a big, loving, God fearing family. It was the values and lessons instilled in her that made her into the strong, loving, and compassionate woman that she is today. She wants to share her story with others so that it can be known that adoption can be a wonderful option for many children who need a home. Jasmine is now pursuing her dreams and jumping hurdles. She currently lives in Mississippi with her family.

Connect with us through PhenomenalJas Enterprise LLC:

Twitter: @phenomenaljas86

Instagram: @phenomenaljasllc

Facebook: PhenomenalJas Enterprise LLC

LinkedIn: https://www.linkedin.com/phenomenaljas-enterprise-llc

Publisher Website: www.phenomenaljasenterprise.com

Business Website: www.phenomenaljasenterprisellc.com

Made in United States
Orlando, FL
09 April 2022

16649227R00095